Wish I Knew Before Loving You
the relationship manual

Dr. Alvin Pelt

Scripture quotations marked NIV are taken from The Holy
Bible, New International Version®, Copyright © 1973,
1978, 1984 by International Bible Society.

Library of Congress Cataloging-in-Publication Data

ISBN: 978-0-692-75836-6

First Printing August 2016

10 9 8 7 6 5 4 3 2 1

Manufactured in the United States of America

Acknowledgments

I would like to begin my acknowledgments by thanking God for sustaining me along an improbable journey through college, medical school, and beyond. I thank you for sending all of the people my way that made this venture possible, and I thank you for allowing me to get to a point in life where I was able to find the time and energy to research the topic and to write this book.

I would be remiss in my duties without a heartfelt thank you to my wife of thirty plus years, Pamela Marie Phillips-Pelt; thank you for staying true to the game during the good times and bad. Thank you for your vision and insistence many moons ago that I should write a book. Thank you for your understanding during the many weekend book meetings and the morning writing sessions while on vacation.

A special thanks goes out to my book project team, including my writing partner, Edie Waugh, who discovered me during a speaking engagement; Chase Broady, my millennial media consultant; Taylor Darden, Graduate student researcher; and to Kevin St. Clair, my fraternal brother, webmaster, and advertising consultant.

I would also like to thank the following individuals who had some influence on the book either directly or indirectly: Judy Barker, principle owner of Barker & Associates and cooperate coach who took the time to work with me personally; Gregory Clay, fraternal brother and visionary, thank you for all your key advice; Focus group attendees, thanks for sharing your personal stories with me; Earth O. Jallow, Columbus, Ohio radio personality and publicist who taught me how to navigate social media; Curtis Jewell, Hall of Famer in Business in Central Ohio, entrepreneur, friend, and mentor, thanks for letting me see over the mountain to the Land of Canaan; My patients, thank you for trusting me with your care and for providing the insight into the relationship dynamics; Book reviewers that took the time to read the manuscript and offered objective criticisms and suggestions for a better product, I thank you.

Elaine Richardson, PhD, author of (*PHD to PhD, How Education Saved My Life*), thanks for helping me get the show started as your co-host at the King Arts Complex in Columbus, Ohio.

Joylynn Ross, author, editor, and literary consultant, thank you for your wonderful literary workshop that was instrumental in getting the book out of my head, and for your professional editing job.

Jerry Saunders, CEO of Afrocentric Personal Development Shop and Columbus, Ohio community leader, thanks for your key advice.

Brian Southers, videographer and consummate professional, thank you.

Terrell Strayhorn, PhD, thank you for conducting my first writers' seminar. Mr. Tai Cornute and the entire staff at the Todd Bell National Research Center on the African American Male, Office of Diversity and Inclusion - The Ohio State University, thank you for inviting me to present the Relationship Seminar at the annual National Black Male Retreat.

A special thanks to my two talented graphic designers, Sophia Do for the logo design and illustrations, and Pannsy Brown of Kenbur Brand Agency for the memorable book cover.

Preface: Wish I Knew Before Loving You

"Indeed, there are many things I wish I'd known about you before falling in love with you." Some of the things may have caused me to make other choices, or at least slowed the pace. If I still chose to stay after discovering some of the things buried deep inside of you, it would have helped me to better understand you; why you felt the way you did, why you acted the way you did. It would have given me some clues on how to help you, or where to send you for help. It would also have helped me to allow you the time and space to heal.

I have practiced clinical psychiatry for over twenty-five years, doing a lot of one-on-one therapy sessions with thousands of patients. Of the three major stressors that lead them into my office (employment problems, finances, and relationship conflicts), I am struck as to how unprepared most people are in the initiating and coexisting in relationships.

I became interested in the area of healthy relationships in 2012 following an invitation to speak on the topic at The Ohio State University's Todd Anthony Bell National Resource Center on the African Male, National Black Male Retreat. In 2016 was my fourth consecutive invitation to present on healthy relationships. I have been pleasantly surprised, delighted, and inspired by the numerous personal questions asked by the men regarding issues with their relationships. The questions and answers following the presentations have morphed into impromptu group therapy sessions. I have also conducted focus groups at my private office, exploring the areas of intimate relationships with various age groups and gender groups.

This book has been written for young to middle-aged men and women interested in initiating and maintaining healthy male-female relationships, and to help them answer some important questions such as the following:

- Who is the right person for me?
- What criteria should I use in selecting a mate?
- How do I get through the drama and trauma that relationships can bring to the table?
- How do I know when it's time to terminate an unhealthy relationship?

How to use this book:

This book should be used as a reference source that gives you some structural guidelines about long-term relationships. I define a long-term relationship as one that has been in existence for one year or more. It should be used like a driver's training manual; a guide that gives you the basic rules of the road, but with the understanding that good driving techniques only come with hours of practice and good advice from experienced drivers.

Chapter One –Anatomy of a Relationship

I. Six Components of a Healthy Relationship:

What is a healthy relationship? It's one that not only gives you the space to grow, but the encouragement to grow. A healthy relationship is one where you can be you, not the actor or pretender of who you think the other person wants you to be in order to stay in the game.

I know it sounds corny, but remember that when you're in a relationship with another person, you are in a relationship with not only their body, but also with their mind. Their mind is a cluster of all their past experiences from childhood, adolescence, and adulthood. It includes their value system, intellect, and personality traits.

A healthy, satisfying relationship is like looking into a fantasy mirror and asking, "Mirror-mirror on the wall, who's the happiest one of all?" This is because being in a healthy relationship makes you feel happy and whole; whole as in complete, intact, and unbroken.

There are six critical elements of a healthy relationship. Let's look at the individual parts:

1. Communication
2. Expression
3. Time Commitment
4. Commonality
5. Trust
6. Respect

To build something suggests that there is a starting point and a finishing point. That is why I refer to growing a relationship rather than building a relationship. Relationships change over time; they require ongoing work in order for them to grow. They need weeding (pulling out the bad parts), watering (keeping it fresh), and pruning (providing shape) for them to continue to grow.

Of all the elements, I think trust and respect are the two most essential ingredients in the growth and maintenance of a relationship. Trust and respect essentially defines whether in fact there is a healthy relationship.

Communication: Communication is our verbal ability to convey thoughts and feelings to others. There can be several barriers that make effective communication difficult. One can be a language barrier. When we speak in different languages, we may have difficulty understanding each other. Another could be accent; we both speak the same language but with such a drastic difference in accent that we find it difficult to understand. Voice tone can also be a barrier. Some people talk so loud that they hurt your eardrums, while some people speak so softly that you miss out on key words in the conversation. The use of abrasive words is another barrier. For example, if you come from an environment where cursing is commonplace and acceptable, speaking with someone from a different background can make you seem offensive. This was the case with me, and it became a critical area of my professional growth. I was fortunate enough to have caring colleagues that clued me in to my poor choice of words, and that helped me make the necessary changes *(I still have occasional slip-ups.).*

Sometimes the barrier is that the other person won't talk, or they have difficulty putting their thoughts and feelings into words. This may cause them to shut down or try to punish you with silence, which is a form of passive aggressive behavior *(if you read the preface, you'd remember that I told you I was a psychiatrist.).*

Expression: Expression is our non-verbal ability to convey thoughts and feelings to others. Facial expressions and body language are very important aspects of communication. Expressions get diluted in electronic media. Texting, Facebooking, and "sliding onto someone's DM's" can all have useful purposes, but what they lack is the ability to convey non-verbal expression. Skype may be an exception to that rule, but it still does not allow you to caress or console the other person. When Skype allows me to hold hands, I will be a bigger fan.

Let's talk more about the impact of non-verbal communication. Think about the various times where words were not the easiest form of communication, such as grieving the death of a loved one, a job loss, or the ending of a friendship. If you are in-tune with your mate, you can easily read their body language and facial expressions, and then offer the appropriate support.

During my graduate school year at Wayne State University, I discovered a study skill technique called the Preview-Review. Part of the technique was to have the student always sit in the first two rows during lectures; close enough that facial expressions could be seen. That way when the professor asked the question, "Is there anyone who doesn't understand?" the student could answer non-verbally, simply with a facial expression (while keeping their self-esteem in-check). Depending on the expression—a confused look versus a nod of the head—the professor would revise his or her previous comments in a simpler form, or proceed on to the next topic.

Time Commitment: Is there a difference in spending time with someone versus spending time around someone? Yes! It takes time to communicate about things we have in common. It takes time to view others' facial expressions (*Facetime*), and it takes a *Time-budget* to initiate and maintain friendships and relationships.

One aspect of time spent in a relationship is what I call *meaningful time*. I believe this requires some conversation and understanding between you and your mate as to what constitutes meaningful time for the both of you. Does this mean giving your undivided attention, your highest level of listening skills, being mentally prepared to listen to a subject matter that is important to your mate, whether that is a deteriorating work situation, a family crisis, or the declining record of a favorite sports team? The answer is yes, yes, and yes.

Many times people miss the point that relationship growth and maintenance is work (*and sometimes hard work*), just like the work that goes into maintaining a beautiful lawn or flower garden. The end result is a beautiful thing, but people don't see the work that went into making it beautiful. I think this is why it is difficult for the Type-A, work driven, multi-tasking individuals to maintain satisfying relationships, unless the other person is highly independent. Take for example Stedman Graham and his relationship with Oprah Winfrey; a relationship that is thirty years and growing.

It is also important to designate a specific time and place to have this meaningful time and to plan to put your work and school assignments down and stay in the moment. It is great when the meaningful time is spent hugging, kissing, or discussing mutually satisfying topics. But remember, there will be times where you will have to put aside your personal needs and step into a purely supportive role.

In the 2013 book titled (*What Are You Bringing to the Table?*) the author, Sheree, discusses the self-assessment of the traits you will need to develop to make yourself a viable asset in a relationship pair. Being able to supply *meaningful time* to your mate is certainly part of the skillset that will set you apart from others and draw your mate closer to you. Consider this; there may be times in your life where you simply don't have the time or energy that is required to engage in an intense and intimate relationship. You will have to perhaps settle for a friendship that does not carry the burdens and responsibilities of a relationship. Communicating this to the other party may be difficult, but it is the mature thing to do.

Commonality: Commonality is the thing that drew us together in the first place, the things we tend to talk about when we get together. Those things can be jobs, dreams, goals, professional shoptalk, politics, culture, the social scene, sports, cash money, travel, or sex.

When I travel abroad, one of the first questions strangers ask is, "Where are you from?" However you answer the question, it can be an "icebreaker" to get the conversation going. But if you mention you're from the same city and state as the other person, it takes you into a deeper, more detailed conversation. "Where in the city do you live?" "Where do you work?" "What type of work do you do?" "Do you know XYZ?" You may end up exchanging contact information to set up a get-together while on the trip.

This is an example of how commonality from a chance encounter can move to a potential association or friendship. It is simply easier to engage in initial conversation where commonality already exists. Those of you that are skilled in the art of "small talk" already know that you can use it to detect areas of commonality with the other person, which is why some people make friends easier than others. The ability to make lots of friends is often attributed to the person's dynamic personality, but it's really the skilled use of "small talk" and the understanding of how commonality can lead to associations, friendships, and possibly intimate relationships.

Trust: *Trust* defined by Merriam-webster.com is faith and confidence in someone as a condition of some relationship; the reliance on the character, ability, strength, or truth of another person. Therefore, gossip, lying, and backstabbing are the equivalent of anti-trust. All are examples of immaturity or pathological personality traits. When detected, you should run as fast as you can in the opposite direction.

Do you have my back? Can I talk with you in confidence? Are you okay around my family? These are important questions that will determine whether a person can get close enough to you to establish a meaningful relationship. It is this lack of trust that destroys many relationships through lying, infidelity, jealousy, money mismanagement, and other anti-social behaviors.

What was not so obvious to me when I first started lecturing on the subject was that for trust to be established, it first has to be given an opportunity and tested out (*a trial run*). For example, do you show up on time for an appointment whether it is a meeting for coffee, or a business pitch? Do you keep things discussed in the conversation or encounter confidential? Can you do what you say you can do, or like the mailman, can you deliver? If so, the other person may be willing to take more risks with you, or take it to the next level, sharing more personal information or start depending on you for support. When you have trust in a person, it allows you to relax your defense mechanisms and feel at ease around that individual. It also makes it more alarming to you when that trust is breached. You experience feelings of betrayal and anger. When there has been a breach of trust, the work of repairing the damage to the relationship is huge, and sometimes impossible.

Respect: And finally, there is respect. In the most basic terms, respect is that which causes you to look up to someone. Sometimes respect is complete, such as, "I admire everything about you." Sometimes respect is partial, limited or segmented, such as, "I admire what you've accomplished in your career, or your service to your community, but I don't care for your political alliance or how you conduct your personal life."

Respect has been established if there is something about you that I admire, if there is something about you I would like to have, or if you're in a place in life I'd like to be.

II. Biology 101: Evolution of mankind; to understand relationships we have to understand ourselves. How did we get here and what makes us tick? The first thing we need to do is look at the brain and how it has evolved and how it functions. We'll start with the old brain versus the new brain, or what is called the reptilian-brain (old brain) versus the mammalian-brain (new brain).

When using these biological terms, I am suggesting that our brains evolved from the reptile brain (scaly creatures) to the mammalian brain (furry creatures). Yes, we were once furry animals; some people still are.

The Catholic Church has spoken-out to address the age old conflict of "how did we get here." It said belief in evolution is not contrary to Christian beliefs. Whether we were made from a mound of clay or whether we evolved from apes into Abraham, it's all a work of God, this is His world, and we're just it.

The old reptilian brain evolved into the middle part of our current modern developed brain, which is called the **midbrain** *(don't get twisted on the biological terminology)*.

The midbrain is the part of the brain that controls our most basic functions, **instincts and emotions.** A simple reptile like a lizard displays both instinct and emotion. The heart is where some people mistakenly assume is the origin of our emotions. In reality, the heart has nothing to do with emotions, it simply pumps warm blood.

The **cortex** is the most recent part of our brain that has evolved. It's the outer part, the spongy part with the squiggly lines (fissures) that we see in most pictures. The cortex controls our thinking or what is commonly referred to as **cognition**, the ability to add 2 + 2 and get 4. In modern day humans (Homo sapiens), the cortex makes up the biggest percentage of our brains *(we've evolved.)*. It gives us the greatest ability for complex decision-making, more capacity than any other animal species. That's why we're "big-headed."

Both of the areas of the brain are vitally important to our survival. Instincts protect us from immediate life-threatening dangers, like how to avoid territories of a lion or a gangbanger. Emotions help us bond to other humans, to feel empathy and provide nurturing. On the flipside, emotions repel us from people that can do us harm. Cognition allows us to think long-term, to think about what is going to happen before it happens, and the ability to play out different scenarios and choose the one that is best. This is called **abstract thinking,** the highest form of intellect. Just for the record, we're all born with some small capacity for abstract thinking. For the most part, abstract thinking is an acquired skill learned through studying mind-stretching subjects like mathematics; algebra and calculus.

Word to the wise; when it comes to choosing relationships, do the math. Expand your ability for abstract thinking so that you can play out the various scenarios in your mind of how a relationship with the person of interest will pan out.

III. Emotional vs. Cognitive Centers: Now that you've completed Biology 101, you should have some basic understanding of what areas of the brain control what functions. Now it's time to look at what areas we use in choosing intimate relationships. I suppose we use both parts. In the very beginning, the meet and greet stage (*hi, how are you doing*), we use the midbrain (the emotional-instinctual part). Oftentimes you can tell whether you like a person within the first few seconds of meeting them. This is most certainly an emotional and instinctual response rather than a rational or logical one.

It is fairly common to make initial decisions based on emotions and surface judgments; things like appearances, sounds, smells, touch, perceptions, etc. However, after we establish some commonality with that individual, we need to use the other part of our brain (the cortex, the thinking part) to decide if this person is good for us in the short-term. Does this person deserve the opportunity to connect with me again? Am I interested enough to exchange contact information? If they pass the "short-term test" and remain in good standing, then we will need to decide later if they're good for us for the long-term and deserve the chance to share our living space, body fluids, and gene pools. Both short-term and long-term decisions should be strictly reserved for the new brain, the cortex (the thinking part).

The reality is that this doesn't always happen. We oftentimes go full speed with the emotions, which are no doubt POWERFUL but sometimes completely UNRELIABLE. We go from the "meet and greet," straight to the sheets, which can be exciting but extremely risky; high risk medically, emotionally, and financially. I suspect many unplanned pregnancies are a result of relationship decisions based on emotion rather than cognition.

Data: 48% of people born in the U.S. were the result of unplanned pregnancies.

Source: A study published in 2011; Centers for Disease Control and Prevention (CDC).

So let's allow the emotions to play, but don't let them have too many drinks, because they may spin out of control and overrule the cortex. Emotions are normal feelings and sometimes they can feel really, really good. So go with the moment for what it's worth, but remember that even during the fun times, good decision-making is vital, so rely on the cortex.

What if it's too late, what if you're already flooded by emotions and can't think straight? People joke about it, but this really does happen. Sometimes we simply are not capable of effectively using our cortex when we're overwhelmed or overcharged emotionally. What should you do in this case? Introduce the new person to a family member or close friend who has your back. They can use their thinking brain (cortex) to help you evaluate the situation. They can be more objective because they are not emotionally involved. They are essentially loaning you their brain (*and eyes*) to help you with your emotional blind spot.

It is good to do this before you move too far into the relationship, but definitely before you move in-between the sheets. By then it may be too late.

To summarize, I advise you to introduce the person of interest to family members and/or close friends soon after the first few dates or encounters. Ask your family and friends their opinion about the person's personality and character. See if they can interpret the intentions of your love interest. Don't take any of their negative feedback personally; remember, they have your back and want what's best for you. They are not blinded by the emotions, the smooth talking, or the sexy appearance *(he's so tall, she's so fine).*

Words of wisdom from my mother: *"All that glitters ain't gold, and everything that looks good to you is not always good for you."*

IV. Freudian Analytical Theory: My goal in this section is to help us better understand our own thoughts, feelings, and behaviors, by teaching some basic elements of Analytical Theory. It is the understanding of the mind and how it works, and how our subconscious thoughts push (motivates) us to behave in a certain way.

Having a better understanding of our own thoughts, feelings, and behaviors enhances our ability to coexist in relationships with other people. It is therefore necessary to have a frame of reference or a model of how the mind works; this is where Dr. Sigmund Freud and his Analytical Theory come into play.

Dr. Freud was a medical doctor that trained in neurology, the study of the brain and nerves. He later became a psychoanalyst and advanced the fields of psychiatry and psychology. A psychoanalyst is a physician or psychologist with advanced training, capable of analyzing a patient's mind and altering his or her personality structure. I briefly considered becoming a psychoanalyst, but it would have taken an additional six years of training on top of the fifteen years I had already put in from undergraduate school, medical school, and psychiatric residency to become a plain psychiatrist. By then I had way too many babies (three) to feed. Hollywood portrays psychiatrists as psychoanalysts; the doctor that has a couch in the office with patients lying down talking about whatever they're thinking.

Freud introduced his version of Analytical Theory in the early 1900s. His initial theory, the Bi-theory (conscious vs. subconscious), preceded his more popular but complex Tritheory, which consists of the Id, Ego, and the Superego.

The Bi-theory, the one I like, simply states that the mind operates on two levels, the conscious and the subconscious, or what I call **The Upstairs** (conscious) and **The Basement** (subconscious).

We are most familiar with the conscious (upstairs) part of the mind because it is the part we use every day, and the part we have control over. What is not so familiar to us is the subconscious part of the mind (the basement); the part that influences us every day, but the part we cannot see or readily control.

The upstairs and the basement compartments are not equal parts. The upstairs represents only about twenty percent of our mind, whereas the basement represents about eighty percent. Think of it as a little green monopoly house sitting on top of a huge basement. Which part do you think is the most powerful?

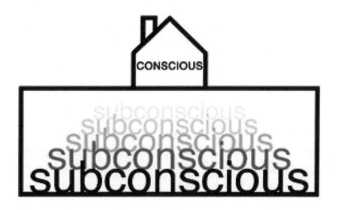

The upstairs and the basement operate on an opposing set of concepts and principles.

The conscious (upstairs) mind utilizes:
- Logic & rational
- Morality

- The concept of time
- Limited memories

In everything we as humans do, we try to do in a logical and rational way, with some concern for morality based on the way we were raised. We also tend to analyze things based on the time frame in which it happened. Conscious memories are limited. If you've ever taken a test, then you know that your ability to remember things has limited capacity (*unless you have a photographic memory*). Sometimes we act in ways that are not logical, rational, or moral. If you've ever committed such an act and then looked back in time and asked yourself, "What made me do it?" some people might say the devil made you do it. Dr. Freud would have said, "No, your subconscious made you do it!"

The subconscious (basement) mind utilizes:
- Instinct & emotions
- The pleasure principle
- It has no concept of time (timeless)
- Un-limited memory

The subconscious (basement) has no use for logic or rational. It operates on instinct and emotion (*think reptilian brain*). It has no use for morality and operates only on the Pleasure Principle; if it feels good, do it. There is no concept of time in the basement. If a distant memory or emotion gets triggered, it feels like it happened yesterday. Our basement stores unlimited memories from our distant past (childhood).

For example: If I asked your conscious (upstairs) mind, "Name something that happened to you in the eleventh grade," it could probably search the memory bank and pull out a few memories from the eleventh grade.

According to Analytical Theory, if I asked your subconscious (basement) mind, "Name something that happened to you in the eleventh grade," it could name me everything that happened every day in the eleventh grade, the seventh grade, the first grade, kindergarten, and preschool; all the way back to the age of two or three. In addition to recording all the memories of every day, it also recorded all the emotions that went along with every memory of every day. This is where things can start to go way wrong.

What I am suggesting is that your past is never really in the past, it's in the basement (subconscious mind). Think about that with the next person you meet and consider getting close to. They are a collection of all the things that happened to them in the past; the childhood, tweenhood, the adolescence, and adulthood. The good things and the bad things. The things they remember *(but may not tell you)*, and the things that their conscious (upstairs) mind has long forgotten, but has been buried alive in the basement.

If you had a storybook childhood, raised by a functional family, had loving parents, had adequate nutrition *(three meals a day)*, safety, warmth, and love, your basement is probably full of wonderful non-threatening memories and emotions. You probably get along fairly well in society, and your self-esteem is probably high. Henry Louis Gates, Jr. once said, "Self-esteem is given in the home." If you had a storybook childhood, you probably have very little difficulty bonding with others and finding satisfying long-term relationships during your adult life.

On the other hand, a childhood experience of abuse, neglect, fear, doubt, food deficits, and shame can create invisible scars in the mind. If you had this kind of childhood, bonding with others and finding satisfying adult relationships will probably be a little more complex. While most people aren't reared in either extreme (we mostly fall somewhere in between), we all experience some troubles in our upbringing that more than likely trigger strange behaviors later on in life that are difficult to explain by simple logic and rational (upstairs concepts). For example, overspending may have very little to do with your love for clothes or shoes, but more to do with your narrow way of boosting your self-esteem or feeling accepted by others. Another example; going through life unable to commit to a relationship for more than a few months may have more to do with your fear of abandonment rather than your desire for multiple lovers.

In my case, I know I'm a super saver because of the deficits I experienced in childhood. My family was a little off (*lights off, gas off, water off*). I can squeeze a dollar until it cries three times. I believe in the saying, "It's not what you make, it's what you keep." Being overly thrifty certainly did affect my relationships because I had a need to control the finances (*to make sure nothing got turned off*). To my spouse, in-laws, and former close friends (*read the chapter on termination*), I must have seemed like a penny-pincher. To resolve these issues with my wife, I had to talk more about the deficits I experienced in my childhood, things I previously tried to hide from her. We finally came to some level of understanding on how her spending habits affected me emotionally (fear), and came to an agreement on how to share resources within the relationship that was mutually satisfying.

When you engage in a long-term relationship, you will eventually get comfortable and relax your defenses, then all kinds of things from the basement will make their way upstairs (*the freak comes out*). They will make their appearances in your emotions and in your behaviors, especially the ones that cause problems and negative reactions from your mate. If you (or your behavior) are being labeled as immature, controlling, or unreasonable by your mate, you might have a basement problem.

These examples demonstrate how surface behaviors can represent much deeper issues from the basement part of the mind. This is why the analytical understanding of behaviors can improve your chances for a successful relationship. This is also why professional counseling is sometimes required to clean out the basement. *(Been there, done that.)*

From this brief lesson in Analytical Theory, one can see that choosing a satisfying long-term mate requires deep thought, detective skills, and the ability to read in-between the lines. It is quite normal for an individual to present the best side of their personality and best personal habits when dating. Your job is to look beyond what is being presented to see what is lying beneath the surface. Use your cortex and its cognitive powers of abstract thinking to look at the various scenarios of how this relationship with this individual could play out (to potentially predict the future). In the chapter "Who do you love?" we will explore the details of how to evaluate a potential long-term mate.

To summarize: The oldest and most primitive part of our brain is the part we share with lower animals such as reptiles. It is called the mid-brain and controls our most basic functions, such as instincts and emotions. The mid-brain is also associated with the subconscious part of our mind (the basement). The most recently developed or evolved part of the human brain is the cortex, the outer part responsible for logical and rational thoughts. The cortex is associated with the conscious part of the mind (the upstairs), the part we have control over.

Chapter Two – Who Do You Love?

I. Crazy Horse:

The number one adult mistake of all times is to hitch your wagon to a crazy horse. The horse may be a fine specimen. He or she might appear beautiful, strong and majestic, but once you start rolling down the road you begin to realize that he is wild, crazy, and unmanageable. He won't stop or turn when you tell him to, instead he starts to bolt out of control, often running off the trail. The wagon starts to bounce high in the air and you start seriously stressing and wondering if you'll survive the ride. You can't enjoy the scenery because you're consumed with anger and fear. Your wagon may eventually overturn with you on it, leaving you "Kind of Blue" just like the Miles Davis CD. Enough said! You can trust me on this one; there are a whole lot of crazy horses running around, and that's coming from the psychiatrist!

Dr. Pelt's advice: Inspect the horse BEFORE you ride.

Let's ask some important questions.

What is the horse's background? Was he beaten and abused as a pony? What is his pedigree? Is he a thoroughbred born to run, or is he a workhorse that is okay just pulling the load? Is he a mixed breed mule, a cross between a male donkey and a female horse, very powerful and strong but stubborn as hell? Is he a wild stallion that is hard to tame?

Has he ever acted crazy in the past? The horse seller may not give you accurate information. They may not see the craziness in the horse because they're crazy themselves, or they might just be trying to sell the horse. You will have to dig for the right information in other places. Just because you ask the right questions doesn't mean you'll get the correct answers.

Does the horse have rabies? Have him checked out by the veterinarian? Does the horse like people *(some do, some don't)*? Does he get along with other horses, or is he a horse hater? Has he ever kicked anybody? If so, how many times? When was the last time that it happened? Did he kick an innocent bystander or was he provoked? What were the events that provoked him?

Don't just attach your wagon to any horse because you want to ride. That wagon may have some valuable goods on it, like your dreams, your future, your babies, or your best shot at financial success.

Consider how difficult it will be to unhook your wagon from a crazy horse. You might get bitten, kicked, or stomped in the process and end up black and blue.

If you've ever ridden a crazy horse, the psychiatrist in me would ask you these questions:

1. Was the horse wild before you met him?
2. Could you tell he was a wild horse from the get-go?
3. Were you so possessed with riding down the wedding aisle that you just needed a horse to ride . . . any horse?
4. Did the horse look so good that you almost wet your pants while waiting to ride?
5. Do you subconsciously like crazy horses?
6. Do you like the thrill and the adrenaline rush that crazy horses bring to the relationship?
7. Do you fear boredom so much that you will reject the thoroughbred or workhorse and jump on a wild, crazy horse?
8. Were your mom and dad crazy horses and now crazy horses seem normal to you? *(Don't blame me, 'cause that's*

all I know).

9. Do you believe that maybe, just maybe you deserve a crazy horse?

A little tip here: You have to know what crazy looks like before you can detect it. That's why we need a baseline idea of what a normal relationship looks like before we can label someone's attitude, behaviors, and belief systems as crazy.

II. Who Do You Love?

One of the most important decisions we make is choosing our mate, and it's done with very little guidance or cognitive input. We use our emotional autopilot. Like the Nike motto, we "just do it." We often do it, as my dad would say, "ass backwards." We fall in love first, and then we try to remake the person into the image we would like them to be. This leads to an inevitable series of fights. *(Get ready to rumble!)*

In other words, we fall into something rather than looking for the right something. In my clinical practice I deal with people every day who've made poor choices when it comes to selecting a mate. *(Talk about life-long suffering…)* I believe that poor choice is also a major contributor to the latest **U.S. divorce rate of 18%.** This data comes from Divorce Rate in the U.S. 2013, SAVE MARRIAGE in the American Community Survey, done by Krista K. Payne at the National Center for Family & Marriage Research (NCFMR), Bowling Green State University. A mistake here can be costly. When things go wrong, it can cause you to become depressed, financially depleted, spiritually challenged, and physically separated from your loved ones.

Recovery from this mistake can take several years to several decades, and sometimes not at all. Choosing a long-term mate requires critical thinking, evaluation, and re-evaluation.

As we move through the chapters of this book, you will develop some ideas of what to look for in a mate to increase your chances of experiencing a happy, healthy relationship. Emotional stability, maturity, and the ability to communicate are the makings of a solid template or outline of a great mate.

III. Don't Waste Your Courtship:

Message to the Men: Both men and women have the mental capacity for cognition and emotion. Women have easier access to the emotional and instinctual parts of their brains. To co-exist with a woman *(happily)*, you have to tap into the emotional parts of your brain frequently to simply understand where they are coming from. *(Yes, you have that capacity.)* You can't interpret every event in the world strictly in terms of logic and rational. If you do, you can be right and wrong all at the same time. You can be technically right but miss out on key pieces of information that causes tension and resentment in the relationship. Using your capacity for emotional awareness is like wearing night vision goggles; you will see things that were there all along but hidden from view by the darkness.

Message to the Women: To co-exist with a man *(happily)*, you have to learn and accept that men do not experience emotions like women. They're not always emotionally immature and unavailable; sometimes they simply don't understand where you're coming from. You can't be emotional with men all the time. It just doesn't make sense to them when you become upset about seemingly trivial things. Sometimes you have to get analytical with a man and say, "Let me analyze this situation. Is it logical or rational for me to feel this way?" If not, deal with the feelings and move on.

Before exclusive dating, we spent most of our time with the same sex friends who thought a lot like us, and then we fell in love.

For better or for worse, your mate will see something in you that very few other people will see; they'll see the real you. The part that's covered over, the part that's been socialized over, the part that you work hardest to conceal. They will, in fact, see the good, the bad, and the ugly.

The good is generally the easiest part to see. Sometimes new revelations will occur, like how you treat your nieces and nephews, or how giving you are to people in need, or how you look-out for the elderly grandparent, uncle, or aunt.

They should also get a glimpse of the bad, the full complement of human behavior that exists in almost everyone. Why do you think they have confession and repentance? For the good, the bad, and the ugly people.

Word to the wise: Don't waste your courtship; you have work to do.

Don't stay up all night on the phone while you get your love fantasy on. Well, it's okay to do that, but you still have work to do (*detective work*). You have people to meet and events to attend. You have to meet the people that raised your mate and the people that were raised with your mate.

Look at old photos, talk to life-long friends, look at old report cards and examine the past grades. Actively listen to the old family stories. Do a timeline of the person of interest. Sometimes *(most of the times)* the stories will be funny and upbeat, but you can still pick out the devilish and the defiance in the core personality of the person of interest, both physically and mentally, as they were growing up.

A person investigating my case would hear about the time I shot my little sister in the leg with a BB gun *(because she pissed me off)*. You'd also hear about the time, at the age of 17, I stayed out late one night partying when my parents went down South for two weeks and left us in the care of my grandmother. They told me they'd be gone for two weeks, but in actuality had only planned to be gone for one week. They came back early and busted me coming home about 2:30 a.m. I can't tell you how many weeks I was grounded, but you could still hear my sister telling those stories during my courtship in my mid through late 20's. *(Payback is a dog.)*

When you discover the good, the bad, and the ugly, does it change your perception of your potential mate? Hope so, because no one is perfect, so when you see the imperfections, you also see the real person. You can make an informed decision on whether you want to proceed with the courtship, or if you want to break camp and run. If you decide to stay, there will be fewer surprises later because you did the investigation work early on. This will give the relationship a better chance of survival.

IV. The Marriage Checklist:

In the book, (*It's Complicated, But Doesn't Have to Be*) by Paul Carrick Brunson, he defines *marriage* as a commitment between two people to live their lives as one.

Mr. Brunson has a check-list of ten questions to determine if you're ready for a long-term commitment called marriage.

Do I Want to:

1. Work on a relationship where the work never ends?
2. Emotionally invest in someone?
3. Be held accountable for my actions?
4. Run my decisions by someone else for approval or disapproval?
5. Care about someone else's day?
6. Share (my toys, money, and my closet space)?
7. Start a family?
8. Sacrifice my time?
9. Sacrifice my personal pleasures?

10. Compromise with someone?

Marriage is the ultimate compromise, for better or for worse, in sickness and in health.

Here are the questions one should ask of a potential mate as it applies to Paul C. Bronson's checklist.

1. Will they work with me (because I am imperfect)?
2. Will they invest in me emotionally; how will they react to me when they're angry with me?
3. What words do they use when they're angry with me; do they sound too much like a controlling mother or father?
4. Can I trust their decisions?
5. Do I love them enough to care about them when *Empire* or the game is on?
6. Are they giving or are they selfish like a child? (Being super fine or handsome looking will not resolve this issue.)
7. Do I trust them raising my kids, even if I'm no longer around (separation, divorce, death, evaporation, or whatever)?
8. Are they worth giving up my team sports, clubbing, or Greek activities?
9. Will they give up ABC to give me XYZ?

Honesty and Truthfulness: Being honest and truthful to yourself and others about what you want from the relationship is essential. Do you like the idea of a future with a variety of options? If so, then don't date someone who wants an exclusive relationship *(unless of course you're a player).*

In choosing a long-term mate, you have to determine if they have the capacity to compromise. *(This calls for an investigation.)*

1. Were they raised as a single child or one of multiple

siblings?
2. Were they the youngest? If so, the ability to compromise may be difficult for them. The youngest sibling or the only child may have overly benefited from the parents' resources and have the least ability to compromise (i.e. spoiled).
3. How many close friends do they have? Long-term friendships involve some ability to compromise.
4. Are they rigid and difficult to get along with in the workplace? Do they go from job to job due to issues with management? Are they well-liked? *(Go to the boring work parties and find out for yourself.)*
5. Have they had other long-term relationships, or are you their first?
6. What were the main factors that caused the end of their previous relationship(s)? *(The best way to study for a test is to look at the old tests.)*

Chapter Three —There Will Be Problems!

I. Men's Brains vs. Women's Brains:

Men's brains and women's brains are different. Men's brains are ten percent larger by volume *(although it doesn't do them much good)*. Men and women have the exact same brain material, but they're wired differently. The difference in the wiring configurations is what distinguishes typical male and female thinking patterns and behaviors. I suggest that this is not a design flaw, but a purposefully executed design by our master designer and maker. As Lady Gaga would say, "We're born this way."

Reference Point: The largest part of the brain consists of two halves called hemispheres, or what is sometimes referred to as the left-brain and the right-brain. The left side is the more analytical side, the side that gets you through school and into a typical packaged job (accountant, nurse, doctor, lawyer, businessman, or businesswoman). The right side is the fun side, the side that is the origin of creativity. It's the part responsible for the artistic you, the funny you, the think-outside-the box you, the part that turns you into Nicki Minaj, Lil Wayne, Dave Chappelle and LeBron James, all at the same time. To connect the dots from the lesson in Biology 101, consider that each hemisphere or brain half is made up of the innermost part of the brain called the midbrain, and the outermost part called the cortex.

A brain cell is called a neuron. It is a long cordlike structure that has multiple connections to other neurons. Think of the brain and its neurons as millions of extension cords connected to one another, connected in a way that conducts electricity to where it needs to go. This is basically how your brain works.

Data: In a 2013 study at the Pearlman School of Medicine at the University of Pennsylvania in the Department of Radiology, Associate Professor Ragini Verma and her colleagues found striking differences in the neuron (brain cell) wiring patterns in men compared to women. This new area of science, the study of brain connectivity, is called Connectomes. The study was published in the *Proceedings of the National Academy of Sciences* in January 2014.

The Differences: The researchers in the Connectomes study found that men have more neuron connections that run from the back to the front within each hemisphere. In contrast, women have more wiring connections that run from side to side, between the left and right hemispheres or brain halves.

Implications: I must warn you that the study of Connectomes is a new science and its clinical implications or applications to everyday life involve some assumptions and risks. More testing and research is needed. It should also be noted that there are individual variations in men and in women that do not fit the typical male or female patterns.

In general, male brains are wired to facilitate perception and coordinate fast actions (rapid response). Men are **"seers and doers."** They perceive a potential problem and jump right on it. Simply put, men make quick decisions and accept the inherent risk that comes with it.

In general, female brains are wired to facilitate communication between the two hemispheres. That allows them to analyze information and utilize other parts of the brain that are responsible for **intuition** when making their decisions. Women perceive a potential problem, have a mental and emotional jolt, and then respond accordingly. Simply put, women are able to utilize more brain functions when making decisions; cognition and intuition.

Intuition defined: [references]
- The ability to understand something immediately, without the need for conscious thought or reasoning [Wikipedia]
- A thing that one knows or considers likely from instinctive feelings rather than conscious reasoning [Oxford Dictionary]
- A keen and quick insight [Dictionary.com]

Women have more advanced verbal skills, memory, and social cognition skills—along with intuition— at their disposal when thinking about problems and making decisions. They will not only out-talk most men, they will get to the right answer faster, which really pisses men off, especially if the relationship is characterized by competition and one-upmanship.

The differences in the way men's and women's brains are wired are meant to be complementary, not inserted to cause conflicts and arguments. Women can see things men can't see right away. They're blessed with a form of Extrasensory Perception (ESP). This can be a set-up for major conflicts. Both men and women can look at the same situation and see totally different aspects. *(Think about the arguments that can cause.)*

This wouldn't lead to conflict if men and women were better informed to understand and respect the differences.

Although scientific research is not yet, and may never be, advanced enough to explain or support it, I believe God *(my belief system)* in His infinite wisdom created us that way, on purpose! Our differently wired brains serve us best when we use them to complement each other, not compete with each other. *(Who knew?)* We're like the Ying and Yang, like ice cream and chocolate syrup, like Batman and Robin; the Dynamic Duo. He created us different, not identical nor with equal parts, but with complementary parts. We're not identical in genetic make-up, physical stature, the way our brains are wired, the way we think, or the way we make decisions.

Men have to reevaluate the way they perceive this. They have to recognize that women's brains are uniquely wired to utilize intuition, and then figure out how to harness it and use it to their advantage (not to take advantage). But first they have to trust it. Once trust in the woman is established, then they can run a real or hypothetical situation past the female-wired brain and get a treasure trove of information and insight.

Think about the times that you sought advice from your mom, sister, grandmother or favorite aunt regarding a conflict at school, work, or a complex social problem. You did it because trust and respect had already been established, the two most basic components of a relationship. There was no competition, verbal put-downs, or I told-you-so's, and you *knew* they had your back. The task at hand is to develop that type of understanding, trust, and respect in your intimate relationships with women.

It only took me thirty-one years of marriage to first understand this, and secondly to appreciate it for what it is. Now I'm taking full advantage of it.

Example: My wife and I were in a meeting with our financial planner, Mr. Carl Buckner of Sestina & Associates. He moved down the projector screen to the next topic of discussion, which was the future sale of my office condo suite. He mentioned there were three ways that could happen: One was the outright sale of the condo with no capital gains tax on profits of under 500K (*certainly not a concern for us*), and the second was a 1031-Exchange where you defer capital gains tax by exchanging one asset (the condo) for another asset that would still generate rental income such as an apartment complex or other commercial property. Before he could finish the explanation of the 1031-Exchange and move on to the third option, my wife jumped in. She mentioned that we were also putting the house up for sale and moving to an apartment. She was ready to move, and all the original neighbors had already moved. This was the optimal time to sale the house, because the interest rates were still low and it would be a good house for another young family because of the large fenced-in back yard and the great school system. I think when she heard the word "apartment" it triggered her multi-line thinking pattern. Every single word of what she'd said was true, but...

Initially, this conversation seemed to be coming from another planet that had nothing to do with the sale of the condo office suite. It previously would have ticked me off because I was still trying to understand and process the information on the second sale option for the condo, the 1031-Exchange, and waiting to hear about the third option *(which, by the way, I never did)*.

This previously would have seemed to be the most obvious, obnoxious, immature, adolescent distraction in a serious conversation between mature adult people. It would have made me view my wife's brain as defective and incapable of following a simple straight line of logical thinking.

Now I can appreciate her advanced cross-wired brain that is capable of entertaining several trains of thoughts at the same time; while still remaining focused on the original conversation. I can appreciate her use of intuition (gut-feelings) in decision making and expressing them in a way that makes totally logical sense to her. My previous reactions would have caused complete confusion for her as she tried to figure out the reasons for my frustration with her seemingly "untimely" and "unrelated" comments.

I now understand and appreciate that a meaningful, productive conversation does not only have to exist in a straight-line, one topic at a time, in a logical sequenced manner, especially when both men-wired brains and women-wired brains are at the table. I can now pick off other important topics as they come out of her brain through her mouth, and that I just have to make some minor adjustments *(honestly, not really that minor)* to my male-wired brain to go with the flow. It's like shooting at a flock of ducks as they land; there are several targets, and they're all tasty.

Same advice goes for women; they have to reevaluate the way they perceive this difference in the brain wiring configurations that distinguishes typical male and female thinking patterns and behaviors. They have to recognize it, understand it, and then figure out how to harness it and use it to their advantage (not to take advantage). But first they have to trust it.

Before a woman enters a serious relationship with a man, she should have checked his background; his family of origin *(Fruit don't fall far from the tree),* his accomplishments, his academic and work history, his criminal record, and his financial standings, including FICA score. If the (FBI) background investigation went well and you signed the contract (apartement lease or marriage license), then you should have some confidence in the man. Hopefully trust and respect has been established. That trust and respect then needs to be extended to his decision making, thought processes, and behaviors, because they are very likely to be different from your own. Know that men may come around to see things as you do, but it may take them longer and require more hard evidence. A wise woman who understands the differences in our thought processes will be able to debate the issues with her mate without frustration or verbal attacks. *(I told you I was right.)* That will allow your mate time to come around to your side and minimize any potential resentment and harsh feelings. Recognizing that you have power is a good thing; learning when and how to use your power is an even better thing.

My wife has made the final decision on our last three residences; two houses and one apartment. I remember the debates *(arguments)* that occurred with each one. She clearly understood when to debate, when to back off, and when to seize the moment and then put the hammer down on the decision. I felt manipulated and lucky all at the same time, because each decision was a win-win deal. She simply saw factors early on that I could not see in real-time. I had to come around later.

GENERALITIES of the SEXES	MEN	WOMEN
TASKING	Single Tasking	Multitasking
INHERENT SKILL SET	Hand-Eye Coordination (hunting, basketball)	Verbal skills (debating, teaching)
THINKING PATTERNS	Tend to rely on hard analytical facts	Utilizes both analytical information + intuition (often relies heavily on intuition)
BEHAVIORAL RESPONSES	Seers and doers: Jump right on things and get them done, but may miss the subsequent ramifications of that action	Analyzers: Decisions can be made without hard facts or logical sequencing, but still come up with the right conclusion and faster (especially when it impacts others)

II. Stress Points:

There are several stress points in every relationship that can cause disruption, decline, or termination. Here are just a few:

- 1-2 years of living together (married or otherwise)
- Having a baby (married or otherwise)
- Increased financial burdens (reality sets in)
- The father becomes jealous of the child

- The mother becomes conflicted and resentful about having to work and care for the child, or leaving him/her at daycare
- Re-alignment of household duties (You expect me to cook?)
- Giving up personal time and personal activities
- When the kids leave (abandon) the house
- Your mate becomes unemployed
- Your mate becomes ill (mentally or physically)
- Infidelity (sneaking, cheating, and back-stabbing)

Nobody's life or relationship is conflict-free *(and I mean nobody)*, so now the question becomes: "How do you deal with it?" One way is to be realistic in your expectations of what lies ahead in a relationship.

Let's look at some common stress events that occur in many committed long-term relationships. Stress points can be positive or negative stressors, for example: We often refer to a new baby as "a little bundle of joy." I call it a little bundle of stress *(a positive stress)*. They are a joy, but they drastically alter all of your life patterns, your sleep-wake cycle, work schedule, shopping schedule, relaxation and downtime schedule, love making schedule *(major changes here)*, and your financial patterns.

Data: "Cost of Raising a Child" report from the U.S. Department of Agriculture *(the people that regulate and set the prices for food)* states that the average cost of raising a child born in 2013 up until age 18 for a middle-income family in the U.S. is approximately **$250,000**. This does not include the cost of college education. *(Don't get me started.)* This amounts to:

a. $13,888 per year for eighteen years or;
b. $1,157 per month or;
c. $578 per two-week pay period or;

d. $289 per week *(Where will this money come from?)*

In anticipation of this major life event, most rational people would delay this event to late twenties or early thirties in order to pay down debt and to save money to finance the "little bundle of joy." Problem is, forty-eight percent of all people born in the U.S. are born un-planned, which allows no time to save. This results in the need for immediate sacrifice, and that becomes a stressful event. That $289 per week split evenly between the two is $144.50 of disposable income that is no longer available for the bar tab, the green fees, the nails, the salon, the weekend get-a-ways, or the mall-madness *(shopping)*.

Another major stress point is **infidelity** (a negative stressor), which is getting your physical needs met outside of the relationship by intercourse (penetration), oral sex, finger sex, and kissing. Getting your emotional needs met by online cheating or a connection with a coworker or friend without any physical contact is also considered infidelity or cheating *(But we were just talking.)*

A 2005 article on Infidelity in Committed Relationships, printed in the *Journal of Marital and Family Therapy* authored by Adrian J. Blow and Kelly Hartnett, reviewed several years of research on extramarital sex. They found that over the lifetime of a marriage or long-term committed relationship, about twenty-five percent of men and fifteen percent of women will engage in some form of extra marital relationship. These relationships may consist of three different types. Sexual only relationships are more common with men. Emotional only relationships or combined sexual-emotional relationships are more common with women.

Over the course of a lengthy marriage or committed relationship, there is slightly less than a twenty-five percent chance that infidelity will occur according to the 2005 study on Infidelity in Committed Relationships. When infidelity in a marriage or a committed relationship does occur, it can lead to mental health problems such as anxiety and depression in the faithful partner. Infidelity is the most common cause of divorce and marital discord in the U.S. Also, 3.3% of all people born in the U.S. are a result of extra marital affairs.

In a 2013 blog post by Susan Walsh, she noted, "The yearly percentage of wives having affairs rose almost 40% during the last two decades to 14.7% in 2010, while the number for men admitting to affairs remained the same at 21%." Her source was the National Opinion Research Center's General Survey.

With more women working fulltime in the workforce, obtaining financial independence, and engaging in social media, they are catching up with the men in the area of infidelity. Emotional affairs tend to have more damaging effects on the relationship and are more difficult to end by the guilty party than a purely physical affair.

The major reason for infidelity listed in the research literature and by online sources is relationship emotional dissatisfaction. Forty-eight percent of men listed this as the reason they stray. Therefore, one can conclude that cheating is not all about sex. When a man forms an emotional connection with a new female, the sex is often a by-product of that new relationship. Women are also more likely to cheat for emotional satisfaction and tend to engage in emotional affairs.

At all cost, you want to monitor your relationship at regular intervals to make sure your mate is not feeling unwanted, undervalued, or taken for granted. Regular dinner outings and going to bed at the same time *(even if you're not sleepy)* will allow you to monitor the situation.

Cheating is a sign *(big sign)* that there is a major disconnect in the relationship. If this was a car, it's time for a major overhaul (couples counseling), not a minor scheduled tune-up. Some people don't do overhauls, they do trade-ins, but sometimes they trade in a Mercedes for a Kia. They both look good, but they're not the same quality.

Infidelity can be (but not always) a major relationship ending event and sometimes lead to battering assault. Some of the known predictors are listed:

- Emotional dissatisfaction with the relationship (#1 Reason)
- Sexual dissatisfaction (Linked to women)
- Narcissistic personality traits or flirters (*It's all about me*)
- History of multiple sex partners (*Inspect the horse before you ride*)
- Prior divorce
- Low levels of religiosity
- Childhood sexual abuse (2007 *Journal of Family Psychology*: Whisman and Snyder)
- Low levels of conscientiousness (See the section on emotional stability)

With several inherent stress points, it's quite apparent that you will need a fairly mature skillset in communication and problem-solving to sustain and survive in a long-term relationship.

In my opinion, **maturity and understanding** are big parts of the success in long-term relationships; being mature enough to understand your role in its success or failure. You have a role to play in your mate's emotional well-being and their level of satisfaction in the relationship, and vice versa. This level of understanding is critical to keeping your mate from straying. It requires some maturity in knowing what pushes your mate away, such as jealousy, nagging, sarcastic condescending statements (words), withholding emotional support and/or physical contact. Remember, the decision to engage in a committed relationship, whether that's monogamous dating, living together, or marriage, can be like a prison sentence if you're not fully ready. Should your mate flip out on you, there are a few options left at your disposal:

- Work it out (which requires two mature partners)
- Act it out with affairs (simply requires availability)
- Walk out (*exit stage left*)

There are some anthropological scientists that believe that exclusive unions (monogamy) are a fairly new evolutionary event, and that this was not a helpful trait of early man. We still have some Mid-Eastern, African, and European societies (*think of the French*) where multiple mates are acceptable.

So keeping this thing together is more than a notion. I believe that having a belief system and value system that incorporate the art of forgiveness and the belief in "doing unto others what you would have them do unto you," is very helpful. It doesn't hurt to believe that the intact family unit is the best way to raise smart, healthy, and emotionally stable children.

As you may have noticed, relationships can have very complex issues. To engage in a healthy relationship, the assumption is that you start with two emotionally mature people that understand the power of words and how to effectively communicate with one another.

How do we measure emotional stability and effective communications in ourselves as well as a potential mate? Read the section on **Evaluation of Emotional Stability** and the Chapter "Failure to Communicate."

III. Mouth Control (Women's Section):

"A woman's greatest assets can be her words; they can also be her greatest liability." -Alvin D. Pelt, MD.

The nursery rhyme "Sticks and stones may break my

bones, but words will never hurt me," is, in the words of my father, a barefaced lie!

Women are the most beautiful beings ever created *(with or without a weave)*, but the ugliest part of her body can be her mouth.

What attracts a man to a woman? Initially, at a glance, it is her stunning God gifted physical features. Secondly, it is her personality, or the person that lives within the body. Thirdly, and most importantly, it is how she can make a man feel about himself. That's where the mouth control comes into play. The words of a woman can build a man up or break him down in a most remarkable way.

A woman does not possess the brute strength of a man, or his voice volume to drown out a conversation, so when engaging in conflict, she resorts to her weapon of choice; words! She is uniquely brain-wired for superior language skills. Her words can be lethal to a man's self-esteem and to the health of a relationship. Her words are just as effective as a strategically placed punch or a body slam. The problem is the resulting damage takes much longer to heal than a bruise or a muscle strain, and the memory of the words can last a lifetime. The choice of words from a woman can change a man's perception of her and his willingness to trust her with his feelings and decision making. Choice of words can create a major wedge in the relationship and inch you closer toward separation and termination. If I was a man, and I am, I would give serious consideration to getting emotionally involved with a woman who has no mouth control.

Voice Tone (nagging): *Nagging* is defined as a repetitive statement, delivered in an abnormal voice tone with a condescending message. Words can be sharper than a kitchen knife; they can slice and dice, or inflict deep wounds. Emotional wounds bleed a long time. They carry a greater

memory-load than other slights, and they make it harder for us to forget and get back to that loving *(Jay Z Empire)* state of mind. Statements delivered with abnormal voice tones, put-downs, and sarcasm will only make one of us feel good (temporarily). It will drive a wedge between the relationship bond, and it allows the evil-one to invade the crack in the space.

One of the main problems in our community, I believe, is that young women are raised without the influence of a great man. If you were never raised by a great man, or raised in the near company of a great man, then how do you know a great man when you see him? To make matters worse, what if a young girl was raised without a man (father) or raised by a bad man? How will she know how to talk to, treat, and appreciate her potential mate? Will she believe and display the attitude that "I don't need a man to be happy or to raise a child?" Will it be trial and error for her? Will it be productive or unproductive? How will she view her mate; as an equal, greater than, or lesser than?

Misconceptions: "We're equals." Who said that? Did God mean for us to be equals? He didn't design us that way; we're shaped differently, men are physically stronger, and women are intuitively sharper.

Men don't want to be treated as "equals," so don't assume that they want that. Men want to be treated special, not as equals. *(Alpha males demand it!)* Men like to feel like they're king of the castle, without having to wrestle for control of it. How can they be your provider *(yes, I know things are changing),* your protector, your confidant, and father to your offspring, and still be seen as your equals?

Advice to the men: *(I know this is the section on women, but the smart men will want to read it.)*

Gentlemen, when exercising your options in the selection

of a woman, here are my recommendations: Select one that is smart, select one that is loyal, then before making the final decision, make sure you examine her choice of words. Listen to what comes out across her lips, because they may be the key to your future, at least in regards to that relationship.

IV. Guilty as Charged (Men's Section):

Guilty as charged! You have been sentenced to several weeks of dry (sex) love making, cold shoulder indifference, uncaring comments, or worse.

Men, by now it should be clear to you why I refer to women as **intellectual/emotional beings**. Their brains are wired differently than ours. Their level of satisfaction in a relationship is based on the fulfillment of the security needs, intellectual needs and emotional needs, not gifts or recent purchases *(although they like those things as well)*. And whose responsibility is it to fill that void? It's no longer her parents' or immediate family members'; it's not her girlfriends' or her "platonic friends'" responsibility. It is yours! So let's talk about how to make that happen and the possible ramifications of what happens when you fall way short of the goal.

Let's face it; most men are brain-wired for the chase *(the hunt and the kill)*, not the capture. Men are **"seers and doers"** *(see her & do her)*. Men get the biggest thrill from the pursuit *(the chase)*. But what happens when you make the decision to kiss the prey and take it home? Well, simply put, you become emotionally attached, and now you have to care for it, feed it, walk it, and play with it (i.e. **nurture** its physical and emotional needs).

Modern-day women are fully capable of nurturing their intellectual and physical needs. They are starting to dominate in the area of academics. The National Center for Education Statistics (NCES) is the primary federal entity for collecting and analyzing data related to education. According to the NCES, every year since 2000, women have been outgaining the men in attainment of bachelor's degrees and higher. 2014 was the latest year the data was analyzed. The percentage of females attaining a bachelor's degree was six points higher than males (thirty-seven percent vs. thirty-one percent), respectively. Similarly, in 2014 the percentage of females attaining an advanced degree (master's degree or higher) was three points higher than the males (nine percent vs. six percent), respectively. Among some racial groups, women exceed the men in degree attainment by two to one in every category.

Women will eventually parlay that academic dominance into dominance in their career fields. Many already earn more money than their male counterparts and have plenty of resources for housing, transportation, pedicures, and shopping. Also, with the new prevalent attitudes in society regarding sex (pre-marital, post-marital or otherwise), it is not too difficult for women to find "friends with benefits" to satisfy their physical needs.

The gaping hole that is left to fill is that of their emotional needs. The American working woman tends to spend more hours per day at work with coworkers; more than with her mate *(especially if he is balling, working-out, or sleeping when he gets off work)*. Unless she is a doctor, nurse or teacher, chances are most of those coworkers are men who may be receptive to filling that emotional void.

How does a man fill the emotional needs of a woman? *(I was hoping you'd ask that question.)* Well, men, you have to become nurturers. Yes, you have to make the switch from the mentality of a predator to that of a nurturer; a major leap in the thinking and behavior of an immature male. This is not to say that men become weak, but they switch to the protector mode. Even the most vicious pit bull will protect the people he lives with. Protecting your woman *(honey, mate, or whatever she is to you)* from the other scavenging males in the environment means to make sure she is emotionally satisfied.

Emotional Needs Course:
- Listening (effectively)
- Spending (meaningful) time
- Offering emotional support (when indicated)
- Playing with each other and having fun
- Building trust (do what you say you're going to do)

Listening effectively: Listening effectively means just that; listening effectively! The way to accomplish that is to rid yourself of the distractions to listening, namely the cell phone, laptop, and flat-screen TV. Even with the sound turned off, I can still get easily distracted by *The Kardashians* and *Love & Hip Hop* (and Facebook is a whole other issue).

Effective listening means the other party "feels" that you have heard them. You may in fact have heard what they said while typing on the cell phone, but they may not "feel" you were listening. Remember you're dealing with **intellectual/ emotional beings,** and her feelings are where it's at. Taking care of her feelings now will result in her taking care of your feelings later *(big time).*

Word to the Wise: Set aside some designated time several days per week to talk *(sorry, I mean to listen; she'll do the talking).* Doing this at a restaurant works well as long as there is no flat screen TV, because Russell Westbrook and the NBA can wreak havoc on your relationship.

To listen effectively, you have to abandon your straight-line, logical sequence thinking *(at least temporarily)* and go with her multi-line thinking in which she will present several different topics simultaneously. *(You have to be focused to do this.)*

"Just let go and go with the flow." It will eventually get easier with practice. Remember, if that opposite sex coworker at her workplace is willing to listen to her, you'd better do so as well. Think of it as protecting your "assets."

Spending time: Spending time *around* someone and spending time *with* someone are totally separate things. I can spend time around someone while studying, doing internet searches, or checking my email and social media accounts, but they may not "feel" I spent time with them. I was physically there but I did nothing for their emotional needs. I did not make much eye-to-eye contact, I did not touch her or console her at the right time *(my hands were busy typing)*, I did not repeat any statements back to make sure I heard them correctly, and I did not offer any constructive input to what was being said, i.e., I was not emotionally available.

Emotional support: This should be a no-brainer. If you care for someone, if you live with someone, if you share body-fluids with someone, then when they're struggling, you should be there to support them. That support means a physical presence and adopting a therapeutic mode where you take on the role of the therapist. This is easier if you've ever been in therapy yourself. You can just use the same phrases the therapist used with (*on*) you. "Tell me more," "I can understand how that made you feel." Or just use common sense and put yourself in your girlfriend or wife's shoes (no, not literally) and offer your support. It may be as simple as hugging her and holding her hands while she talks through her pain.

Typical things that tend to stress her and cause her emotional pain (in no particular order):
- Ending a friendship (has more impact with women than with men)
- A new or chronic medical problem

- Miscarriage
- Death of a family member
- Job stress (has turned her into a weekend girl, no time during the weekday)
- Job loss, or denied a sought out promotion
- Advancing age (and you still haven't set a commitment date)
- Financial set-backs
- Extended family issues
- Abundance of responsibility due to over committing herself to others and projects

Playing and having fun: Why bother with the whole relationship thing if it's no fun? We can just become serial daters and skip out on the trauma and drama that comes with committed relationships. We'd also miss out on the consummate experience of living in the same house and watching our children grow and mature, and knowing that you have someone that's got your back when you go down physically, financially, or legally. We know there will be problems in every relationship. There will be bumps in the road and crashes into brick walls, but for now, let's have some fun!

I personally believe that the more fun you have as a couple, the more relationship capital you have to spend when times get rough and the relationship is on the edge. How easy is it to ditch someone that you've shared major fun moments in life with? Fun moments like the driving trips, the cruises, the visits to the zoo, the surprise birthday celebrations, the concerts, and hanging out with friends. These are memories that are hard to erase when considering starting over in a new relationship.

Building trust: Nothing says that you are "the man" like following through on what you say you will do. Everyone respects that, males and females alike. Once a woman knows she can trust you and that you have her back, you are in fact meeting one of her most basic emotional needs, that of security. She can count on you to be there for her. Keep in mind that this was once the responsibility of her (functional) father if she had one, and this can be a rather difficult role to fill. For some men it takes rearing their own daughters before they can truly understand a woman's basic need for security. However, you'll be better off trying to understand this before having kids. Remember, there's a 50/50 chance of having a boy. I had three . . . And no girls!

V. Emotional Stability:

How do we, and why should we, evaluate a potential mate's emotional stability? This is a major factor in determining the health and life of a relationship.

People with a **high level of emotional stability** are less likely to experience negative emotions like anxiety, anger, envy, guilt, and depression. They are cool under pressure and are easygoing. They are generally described as laid back. *(This is the type of horse you want to hitch your wagon to.)*

People with a **poor level of emotional stability** tend to respond poorly to life stressors. They are more likely to interpret common everyday situations as negative and threatening. They experience minor challenges as overwhelming events. They are more likely to experience life as stressful *(and to go off on you and others)*.

An emotionally mature individual is able to follow through on tasks and complete projects. They will leave a paper trail of their accomplishments and of their ability to overcome obstacles and challenges. They will have meaningful connections with other people, varied interests, and ample social skills *(the most interesting man in the world)*.

On the *Big Five Model of Personality Assessment Tool,* which is used by companies for hiring and promotion purposes, there are five areas of an individual's personality to be evaluated:

1.   Emotional Stability refers to one's proneness to negative emotions such as anxiety, anger, envy, guilt, and depressed mood.

2.   Extraversion refers to the number of relationships that people have (one friend vs. twenty). High extraverted people have a large number of friends and spend a large amount of time enjoying them. Less extraverted people have a smaller number of friendships and spend a smaller amount of time with those friends.

3.   Openness refers to the number of interests to which one has and the depth to which those interests are pursued. Highly open people have many interests and, consequently, less depth within each interest (i.e. they do a lot of things, but don't spend too much time on any one). Low openness refers to a person with relatively few interests but spends relatively more time with those limited interests (at church all the time, only spends time around family).

4.   Agreeableness refers to a person's willingness to interact with other people. Highly agreeable people respond to others with warmth and try to avoid conflict. Low agreeableness describes people who do not play well with others.

5.   Conscientiousness refers to goal-directed behavior. Highly conscientiousness people are able to focus intensely on their goals and exhibits self-discipline. Low conscientiousness refers to people who are disorganized and distracted. They exhibit poor self-control (over-eaters, over-spenders, serial cheaters). When evaluating a person as a potential long-term mate, you should do some critical evaluation. Let me break it down for you:

     a.   Look at their resume; it should give you a good listing of their accomplishments.

     b.   Do the "wallet biopsy" *(you know I'm a doctor)*; their savings account, credit card balance, and Experian credit report will let you know if they can control their impulses. (Can you trust them with money?)

     c.   The high school and college transcripts will let you know if they are a focused, a task-oriented individual is capable of following through and completing goals. These traits will be apparent early on in life. You don't have to wait until they're 30 to see if they'll mature.

     d.   The legal record (can be found with an online search) will let you know if they can get along with other people and are able to conform to the expected norms (or are they a menace to society). Warning; check the fruit on the tree. I know angry women who have set cars on fire *(yes, I really do)*.

     e.   Find out how many trips have they taken to rehab *(one should be plenty)*.

Remember, you can fall into a relationship with someone *(fantasy life)*, or you can develop a template of the type of person that will be good for you and use your cognitive (upstairs) brain to check the fruit on the tree and determine if they are a good match for you. *(Do you like crazy horses?)*

Chapter Four – "Failure to Communicate"

I. Introduction:

In the 1967 big screen movie, "Cool Hand Luke," actor Paul Newman *(yes the same guy whose picture is on the salad dressing bottle, whose company, "Newman's Own," donates all profits to charity, who is from Cleveland, Ohio and went to Kenyon College)* played a rebellious inmate, Luke Jackson, at a southern prison where he would escape time after time. The law would always find him and drag him back, beat him, and then put him in solitary confinement. The warden would make an example of him to the other inmates and issued his immortal line, **"What we've got here is a failure to communicate."**

Your relationship will suffer a lot, just like Cool Hand Luke, unless you figure out an effective way to communicate with your mate. Conflict resolution demands effective communication.

II. Communication is the Key:

In the chapter, "Anatomy of a Relationship," we looked at the six-basic components of a relationship. It is the **trust and respect** that determines if there is enough soil, water, and sun to grow a budding friendship into something long-term. But it's the **communication** that determines if there is enough fertilizer and weed killer to grow it into a strong, mature, and healthy plant to weather all the impending storms.

In the previous chapter, "There Will Be Problems," it conveys that there will be challenges in every relationship, just like there is in every growing season (drought, pests, and bad weather).

Relationships and life in general have some similarities;

they are like driving a car. Most of the ride is on smooth road *(hopefully)*. It doesn't take much effort to keep the car in between the lines while driving on smooth road *(at least for an experienced driver)*. You can drive with one hand on the steering wheel while talking with your passenger. But with relationships, just like real life, you will eventually hit some bumps in the road; then it will become much more difficult to keep the car in between the lines as it starts to fishtail in the back.

The first thing you do is grab the steering wheel with both hands, gripping real tight. You're trying not to get run over by the semi-trucks in the next lane that will not even slow down. You may hit another stretch of smooth road where the driving *(and the loving)* becomes much easier, but if your life and your relationships have been anything like mine, you know you're eventually going to hit more bumps in the road or smack into some brick walls. When the car hits the brick wall, the impact will cause it to flip three times and you will end up in left field. You may knock down a tree or two or take-out a farmer's cow. *(He's going to be real pissed in the morning.)* It will take AAA to tow your car back onto the road.

When—not if—you hit the bumps in the road and the brick walls in your relationship, it's going to take a real mature level of communication and problem-solving to get the relationship back on track and rolling in between the lines. There is just no room for an immature, juvenile skillset here. This is the adult program! The pouting, yelling, word-assaults, silent treatments, and acting out has no place here. It will not get the job done. Your mamma can't fix this; your daddy's money won't make this go away. You will have to man-up/ woman-up or you will be another relationship roadside causality.

III. The Problem with Keeping It Real:

So you thought expressing your views exactly as you see them, without constraints, would be helpful to your relationship? That it would somehow cause a behavioral change in your mate? How naive.

The problem with keeping it real is that when people hear anything from you that sounds like criticism, they tend to:

a) Become defensive (stop listening to you)

b) Counter-attack you (with their own come-backs)

c) Have less love and respect for you

The criticism may come in the form of a nagging voice tone, a verbal put-down, or a sarcastic comment or joke *(words, words, words)*. Negative comments are usually the result of frustration and irritation we have toward our mates. We are attempting to facilitate a change in their behavior or attitude *(in a most inappropriate way)*.

Most of us learned or adopted our communication style from modeling. Modeling is a very basic learning technique. It is the one you used when learning to speak English, way before you could say your ABC's. That modeling came from our parents, the folks that raised us. I've already quoted comments in the book that came straight from my dad's mouth: "barefaced lie" and "ass-backwards." I'm really careful not to use them in my relationship disputes. Many of us modeled negative behaviors because that's what was presented to us. Unless you've taken a relationship course *(you're currently in that class)* or came from a generation of functional families, you probably have been exposed to bad modeling. In that case, you will have to unlearn the bad habits and adopt some healthier ones.

We all look for Mister Perfect or Miss Right, someone with the right look, the right financial standing, and the right emotional (stability) temperament. Truth is, there is no one ready-made perfect for you. *(Soulmate? Forget about it already.)* Once you've had your first big blowout, what is known as the "Post Honeymoon Syndrome," everyone's breath starts to stink. True there are some people that are more compatible for you than others, but there will always be some areas where you are not compatible.

Being able to express your needs and concerns without coming across as blaming or criticizing, while still being receptive to the other person's needs, is the key to effective communication. The more skillful you are at this mode of communication, the more likely you are to keep your mate by your side (and the fewer apologies you'll have to make).

Constant Reminder: Effective long-term, loving relationships yield higher financial benefits and better physical and emotional health. They also yield smarter, higher achieving, and healthier children.

IV. Effective Communication:

A failure to communicate is essentially a failure at problem-solving. One party may try to dominate the other by their emotional power. The other may resort to passive aggressive behavior where they do something subtle and seemingly unrelated that they know will tick you off.

The failure to communicate and solve the original problem can lead to other destructive behaviors and potential deal breakers like verbal put-downs, sabotage, backstabbing, and cheating. These types of behaviors often disrupt the love flow, the peace, the ability to comfort each other and the kids. This is what I call the "Anti-love." Now you start seeing and expecting the worse. You lose the healing properties of human touch and the calming effects of sexual orgasm. You harbor anger and resentment, start second-guessing *(I should have made a different choice)*, and begin looking for alternatives.

After several days or weeks pass in this relationship battle, the anger starts to subside and clearer thinking emerges. Remorse and loneliness may give way to rational conversation, apologies, and reconciliation. You may start to build a bridge back toward each other, however, the two land masses may never come back together completely. The prolonged battle may allow some trust issues to surface, resulting in fear of disclosing your real feelings to your mate. You may start to feel that you have to watch your back instead of feeling that your mate "has got your back."

Communication Techniques:

1. **Head Check**-Recognize and label the negative feelings you're experiencing (anger, resentment, hurt). Cage it before speaking on it or acting on it. *(Deep breathing may be helpful here.)* Remember, once your words enter the airspace, you can't pull them back; they will reach their target like a launched rocket.

2. **Verbalize the Emotion**-In a calm way. Express your thoughts to your mate by connecting their actions to the emotions you are feeling. Remember, they are never responsible for your feelings, but perhaps their behaviors are a trigger for them.

3. **Wait for a Response**-Allow your mate to respond without being up in their face. Make sure that what you were feeling was accurate based on what you were seeing or hearing *(or what you thought you saw or heard)*.

4. **Give Positive Feedback**-By instructing the other person how to respond to you. "I'd appreciate if you didn't do XYZ. It whacks me out." Basically, you're telling the other person how their actions and behaviors affect you. Coexisting and cohabitating

requires collaboration and negotiation. It requires
some give and take, and learning how to create
positive mental space for your mate.

5. **Test the Water**-Now that you've given the other
party some instructions and feedback, see if the
lesson takes hold. It will generally take more than
one instructional attempt to effect behavioral change
in another person; however, if they love and respect
you, they'll want to please you. It takes time. If after
repeated attempts there is no change in the behavior,
you may be looking at a deal-breaker or a third party
intervention with a counselor.

V. Conflict Resolution:

What is normal? It is normal to have disagreements
and arguments. When you form a long-term union,
you're blending the ideas of two people who were raised
in two different households with different operating
systems; different relationship influences (male vs. female
dominance), different child rearing practices (corporal
punishment vs. free-will parenting), and different ketchup
placement systems (the refrigerator vs. the cabinet).

There are several thousands of differences in each
person's upbringing; most of those will require some level
of debate or argument to settle on the one that works for
the new union. That means several thousands of debates or
arguments to work this out, so get used to communicating.

Some levels of heated debate/argument can be healthy
for a relationship, but always be mindful not to allow it to
escalate out of control, which can lead to abusive behaviors.

Side Note: It's NEVER okay to verbally, emotionally,
psychologically, or physically hurt, attack, or abuse anyone
(I'm talking to both men and women here), so don't even consider

doing it to the one you say you "love."

My Mother's Advice: "Son, if you have a woman who you feel you have to put your hands on, then you need a new woman."

Chapter Five – Terminator

I. Introduction to Terminating a Relationship:

Everyone will experience some setbacks in their long-term relationships; that will start an evaluation process of the worth of the relationship, the risks versus the benefits. If it has positive value, then naturally you will try to save it.

Sometimes when you've exhausted all of your options— spousal parenting, empathy, patience, prayer, begging, threatening ultimatums, second, third, fourth, and fifth chances, failed attempts to overlook the problems (denial) and therapy, etc.—you'll finally come to the conclusion that you have to vacate, have to eliminate, and have to terminate the relationship *(not the person)*!

There are several termination techniques. Some are more mature than others. Some techniques tend to create long-term enemies and others may create long-term friendships. I remember several years ago asking a divorced patient, "How will you get home from the hospital and manage things for the next few days?"

He said, to my surprise, "I'll call my ex-wife." When he recognized the confusing look on my face he went on to say, "Doc, my ex-wife is now my best friend. She'd do anything for me. We get along much better since we divorced."

Apparently this was a relationship that ended well, and they were willing and able to maintain a new connection that was mutually satisfying for both.

Post-Relationship Goal: Once you've tried to repair a broken relationship and then determined that it was time to cut your losses, I think it is helpful for you to consider what the "Post-Relationship Environment" will look like. Once you have an idea (realistic or not), it will give you some notion of which termination technique to use. Is this a really good person, but just not the right one for me (at this time)? Was there a major breach of trust and respect and you'd rather not be friends going forward?

Is this person (male or female) anti-social and dangerous, and caution needs to be a factor in the equation? Is the person emotionally unstable and is at risk of harming themselves or others?

Depending on the depth, length, and intensity of an intimate relationship and the reason for its termination, it can be difficult to turn it into a decent, respectable friendship. It will take maturity on the part of both parties, and it will require newly established boundaries and time; time to resolve the lingering residual intimate feelings. It will take time to heal from the relationship and to move on. You know you've moved on when you genuinely wish the best for your ex-lover and/or have formed new satisfying intimate bonds with other people. This timeframe is usually measured in months, not days or weeks. Trying to change an intimate relationship into a platonic relationship (friendship) while one or both parties have unresolved feelings is a prescription for disaster! *Platonic* is defined in the Cambridge American English Dictionary as a relationship that is loving but not sexual.

What is the difference between friendship and a relationship you might ask?

People in intimate relationships are emotionally involved and have romantic attachments. A friendship is involvement with a person whom one knows, likes, trusts, and has bonds of mutual affection, but is typically exclusive of sexual or family relations.

II. Termination Techniques:

Some techniques are more mature than others. The one you choose may be a reflection of your maturity level, or the depth or nature of your relationship.

The main thing to consider is **The Golden Rule:** *"Do unto others as you would have them do unto you"* (Luke 6:31 NIV).

If I were being broken up with, I'd at least expect you to first, inform me, and secondly, to give me a reason why; these are the two most basic aspects of ending a relationship. To do otherwise would leave me wondering why; was it something on my end, something on your end, or a combination of the two? It would also make me feel less than a whole person since you're terminating an emotional connection with me without defining the end-point or stating the reason why. You'd leave me hanging while I'm still under the impression that we're an item, but you have moved on. Ending the relationship this way could certainly cause me to lose respect for you at the very least, and possibly harbor long-term resentment and anger toward you.

The ending of most relationships are painful but offer potential valuable lessons to be learned; things that I may be able to change the next time around, or insight in choosing a better mate.

Blowing a good relationship also helps us mature into "Fully Actualized Adults" *(one of my favorite 1970s pop psychology terms)*. Self-actualization involves fulfilling your potential and being all that you can be. The concept was conceived by American Psychologist Abraham Maslow in the late 1950s/ early 1960s. Self-actualized people not only fully accept themselves, but they also embrace other people for who they are.

Informing me that you are ending our relationship, and offering a reason why, is actually showing respect for me and concern for my well-being. It also establishes the post-relationship environment; will we consider an attempt to be friends down the road, or will we just kiss and say good-bye?

When you end a relationship in a mature way, you invite less anger, resentment, and retribution on behalf of the departing party.

My two most memorable break-ups *(where I was the terminee not the terminator)* occurred early in life, thank goodness.

The first was a high school romance with an older woman. She was eighteen and I was sixteen years old *(barely legal)*. She'd gone away to college during my senior year and never called again. The phones were still attached to the dorm walls back then, and apparently she was never near the wall or was too tired to get up to answer the phone. I was devastated and was left on my own to draw the right conclusions about the status of the relationship. Thankfully, I was smart enough to figure it out quickly and started the grieving process. I felt disrespected because she didn't have the decency to tell me it was over.

The second break-up occurred during my sophomore year in college, with my freshmen year sweetheart. We thought we were definitely in love, but the absence during the summer break was brutal and essentially fatal on the relationship. I wanted the relationship to continue, but she pulled the trigger on it and killed it dead. The thing that helped me regroup was that she communicated her desire to end it at that precise moment in time, and offered detailed reasons as to why. *(Both parties were guilty as charged.)*

Termination Techniques (Immature to mature forms):

1. **Stab to the Heart:** This termination technique is used with the premeditated intent of inflicting pain on the other party. It is a very immature way of exacting revenge. "This is payback for the pain you caused me." A typical example is where you start seeing someone else

before you've officially ended the previous relationship and they find out about it. "You found out, oh well . . ."

2. **Drop-out:** "Exit stage left." This is where you simply disappear from the scene; no phone calls, no text messages or instant messages, and you've blocked the phone from incoming calls. There is no communication what-so-ever. This technique is typical for narcissists who have feelings only for themselves, or sociopaths who have no feelings at all (*cold as ice as Rick James would say*).

3. **Second-hand Notice:** You've told everyone that the relationship is ending or has ended; that is everyone except the other party. They found out by someone other than you. It does not matter whether you intended for it to happen this way or not. You fumbled the ball and lost the game. You should never end a relationship by setting someone else up to do the dirty work for you.

4. **The Fade Away:** This is where you reduce the frequency of phone calls, texts, and face-to-face contacts in hopes that the other party will become disinterested and drift away. This method is actually grounded in behavioral science. It involves extinguishing a particular behavior; in this case, the behavior of loving you. It sometimes backfires, as the other person notices the distance you've placed between the two of you and starts to grab-on tighter because they feel you slipping away.

5. **Written Notice:** This is where you begin the process of formally ending a relationship with an official notice, in this case a written one. The written notice has several advantages. Writing a letter is a typical counseling-therapy technique used to get in-touch with your real feelings and to get them out through the process of writing. When writing the termination letter, you get

to edit and revise it to say exactly what you want it to say. You can take several days to get through the process. You can choose to send it or deliver it at the most optimal time. Be considerate of the delivery time. Don't do it when the other party is most burdened, such as right before an examination or at the beginning of their work week. Allowing them some down-time (weekend) to collect themselves and express their emotions is really a decent thing to do.

6. **Let's talk about it:** This is a cool method to use when you have two emotionally stable people that may want to become future friends. You agree to meet at a neutral place to discuss the relationship. I always like to have my words written down on paper before I have a difficult conversation with someone. It allows me the opportunity to rehearse it beforehand and to get straight to the point without the emotionality. It also helps keep me on track. Keep the termination conversation short; the other party will not remember much anyway after you say you're ending the relationship. List the reasons why you're ending it. You don't need to justify your position or argue the point. Simply say you've come to that conclusion or made the decision that you think is best for you at this time. It's okay to wish them well and indicate if you'd be interested in being friends down the road *(regular friends, not the platonic kind with underlying loving feelings that are not expressed on the surface).*

Once you've notified the terminee (your now ex) that the relationship is over, it's important to cut the emotional connections (as best as you can). You have to stop any ongoing conversations for a while until you both heal emotionally, that includes instant messages *(I miss you 2)*, text messages, phone calls *(if that still exist)*, Facebook posts, or whatever is the latest means of communication.

Return their belongings and other shared items (the dog or cat). You need to delete the email address and his/her phone number from your contact list (just in case you get weak). Delete the birth date reminder from your Gmail calendar. *(Please do this.)* Deleting old pictures from your cellphone is a no-brainer unless you want your heart to bleed-out or you're really into pain.

"Sticks and stones may break my bones but chains and whips excite me. I like it, like it." Rhianna – "S&M" (2011)

III. Terminating in a Dangerous Situation:

Terminating in a dangerous situation is not the same as ending a normal relationship. When you've encountered intimidation and threats of violence (assault), or actual battery on your person or destruction of your property, then you know you've made a serious error in choosing this person to enter into a relationship with. Here come the sayings. You didn't check the fruit on the tree. Hindsight is 20:20. I *Wish I Knew Before Loving You.*

Black's Law Dictionary Seventh Edition defines *assault* as the threat or use of force on another that causes that person to have a reasonable apprehension (fear) of imminent harm. For example, "I will kick your ass." It defines *battery* as the application of force to another, resulting in harmful or offensive contact. The acts of spitting on a person or kissing without consent are two examples of battery.

When dealing with a potentially volatile or dangerous person (one that's going-off, or threatening to), you should not do a one-on-one, face-to-face termination. Termination by letter, text, phone, or email will be acceptable alternatives under these circumstances. Immediately prior to this type of termination you should inform others of your intent, so that if an unfortunate event occurs, you have others to verify the triggering event. The actual news should still come from you, not the informants.

If you do decide to do a face-to-face termination, take someone with you! If you have doubts or fear for your safety, ask for a security escort from the police or hire a bodyguard. While this may seem costly and extreme, in this case, an ounce of prevention is worth a pound of cure. A police escort or bodyguard also sends a clear message to your ex that it's over; the relationship, the intimidation, the abuse. Please note; I am not talking exclusively about abusive men. Women can be just as hostile and abusive. Think about all the keyed cars you've seen. When you have professional aspirations, whether they are for professional sports or the practice of medicine, you cannot afford to get entangled in the court system and judicial system.

Make this termination short and straight to the point. Indicate that you want no further contact. Do this in writing and keep a dated copy to verify the date that the relationship terminated and your requests for no further contact.

You also have to hold it down on your end with no further contact. Just because you ended the relationship this week won't mean you're safe next week. Inform others around you that you have safety concerns. Move about in numbers for the next several weeks. Don't drag an innocent bystander into the mess by starting a new relationship when you have unresolved issues from the past one. It is probably prudent advice to stay vigilant at least for the next three months, to allow your ex time to resolve her/his *(done on purpose)* feelings of anger and resentment.

IV. Now That It's Over:

"When I think about you, my feelings can't explain why after all this time my heart still feels pain..." "Saturday Love" - Duet by Sherrelle & Alexander O'Neal, written by James Samuel "Jimmy Jam" Harris III & Terry Steven Lewis.

Now that it's over, how do I stop the pain? We are a combination of mind, body, and spirit. We are emotional beings *(yes, men, I'm talking about you too)* and when we experience losses, we experience pain, emotional pain.

One distinguishing feature of human beings is that we form life-long bonds. Very few animal species share this trait, elephants and dolphins are two examples. When our human-human bond ends, we are impacted emotionally . . . And feel the pain in our mind, body, and spirit.

That emotional pain can range from sadness with inability to eat, sleep, or experience pleasure for days to weeks. On the opposite end of the spectrum, we can become "clinically" depressed with the inability to function at home, work, or school.

In rare cases, termination of a relationship can lead to suicidal thoughts or suicidal gestures (cutting, overuse of alcohol and drugs, reckless driving). It can also lead to homicidal thoughts and aggressive behaviors. If you've reached this point, a mental health evaluation, counseling, and/or medication are definitely in order.

For most people, the sadness and loneliness will gradually subside over time, measured by days to weeks. During the resolution phase, chicken and shrimp will start to taste good again, and going out will become exciting again. It may take extra time and effort, but keep in mind that ending (terminating) a relationship that wasn't right for you will clear the playing field to meet someone who is right for you.

The experience of initiating and terminating relationships is an important part of the process of maturing and long-term mating. The lessons learned from one initiation-termination experience can carry over to subsequent relationships. After it's over, it's important to take good care of yourself. Don't isolate for more than a couple of days.

Let your friends know that your schedule is open. I had a friend that posted on Facebook that his marriage had ended and that he has shared custody of his daughter. Get back to the gym or the Pilates class. Increase your productivity at work and school. Rededicate your time to some spiritual growth and healing.

These are the things that will help build you up mentally, physically, and spiritually. They will also increase your self-esteem and sense of well-being and allow you to rejoin the human race!

Afterword

One universal aspect of the human experience is the desire for companionship. The most intimate form of companionship is that of a mating partner. We are greatly affected by this important choice. With the complexities of our modern society, it has become more difficult to determine the best means of the selection of a mate.

Understand that the person you see during the courtship is just a shadow of the real person, or as Chris Rock stated, *"When you meet somebody for the first time, you're not meeting them, you're meeting their representative."* It is imperative that we look beyond the surface during the courtship. We must look beyond the blinding emotions of love and infatuation in order to explore a potential mate. Explore the background, personality makeup, and value system to get a glimpse of the real person; the person that is concealed far below the surface.

This exploration phase should extend far beyond an Experian credit report and FICA score. It should include the family of origin and the dynamics and experiences of childhood, adolescence, and early adulthood. It should include the gender dominance of the family of origin to determine which parent was the most influential and made important decisions for the family. This exploration should also include the prior experiences of entitlement, abuse, abandonment, or neglect.

My hope is that you can appreciate the hidden, and sometimes subconscious, influences from the past and how they play out in everyday events of our lives when we are involved in close, intimate, long-term relationships.

It is critical to recognize your own influences on the success or failure of a relationship. Development of communication skills and emotional maturity are the vital nutrients that allow a relationship to grow and thrive.

It would be naive to assume that all relationships will last until the grave; many of us will have to reboot and start new relationships over the course of a lifetime before we find one that is satisfying and permanent. This necessitates the need to understand and master the skills of initiation, maintenance, and the termination of a relationship. Possession of these skills will allow you to spend less time in withering relationships and to exit wisely. The weeding of the field provides space for new seeds to be planted and for new growth to occur.

There are no ready-made perfect people. Loving someone and forming a mating bond is a process, oftentimes enjoyable, but always demanding and labor intensive. Embrace the challenge common to all mankind; one that has been with us from the beginning and will remain until the end of time.

About the Author

Dr. Alvin D. Pelt currently resides in Columbus, Ohio. He is a native of Lagrange, Georgia. He was raised and educated in Detroit, Michigan. He received his Bachelor of Science degree in Biology from Western Michigan University in Kalamazoo, Michigan, and his Medical Degree and Psychiatric training at Wayne State University School of Medicine in Detroit, Michigan. He serves as a board member for the Western Michigan University Alumni Association.

He has 27 years of experience in the field of clinical psychiatry and serves as Clinical Assistant Professor of Psychiatry at The Ohio State University department of Psychiatry and Ohio University college of Osteopathic Medicine.

Dr. Pelt has conducted focus groups and lectured extensively on various topics related to healthy relationships with the primary focus on intimate relationships. You can reach out to the author by visiting his website at www.therelationshipmd.com or emailing him at apelt@therelationshipmd.com.